## ABOUT THE AUTHOR

**Lorna Rose** has been on the UK po
is a slam winner and has headlined various acclaimed nights such
as Hit the Ode and Jawdance, toured with Apples and Snakes and
performed at festivals like Glastonbury, Ledbury, Shambala and
Moseley Folk. Her poems have been published in Amethyst, High
Window and Anansi Archive. She directed Ten Letters, an
intergenerational poetry show about Birmingham and was part
of the Decadent Divas and the New October Poets collectives.
She is also an actor, playwright, podcaster and co-creative
director of RoguePlay Theatre. She has three poetic spoken word
solo shows under her belt, poems from which can be found in
this collection.

You can listen to her work here: https://soundcloud.com/
lornarosepoet

Rebel Heroines Podcast (Celebrating the women of Greek
Mythology) https://podcasters.spotify.com/pod/show/rebel-
heroines

Twitter: @rebel_heroines

# Lorna Rose
## Caterpillar Soup

**VERVE**
POETRY PRESS
BIRMINGHAM

PUBLISHED BY VERVE POETRY PRESS
https://vervepoetrypress.com
mail@vervepoetrypress.com

FIRST PUBLISHED MARCH 2024


Printed and bound in the UK
by ImprintDigital, Exeter


ISBN: 978-1-913917-50-0


Cover Design by Clare Tedstone
www.instagram.com/clairetedstoneart/

*This book is dedicated to
the sister who helped me grow,
the rock star who made me wild
and the man who changed my life*

# CONTENTS

**SACRED**

**A VIRGINS GUIDE TO HIRING AN ESCORT**

## COSMOS

*Acknowledgements, Thankyous*

# Caterpillar
# Soup

Mona Rose x

*Before a caterpillar becomes a butterfly, it disintegrates inside the chrysalis into a liquid known as caterpillar soup. Somehow, this substance instinctively knows how to transform into something beautiful, that for its brief life, can fly.*

# Brazen

*For Jim Morrison*

# Fantasy Meeting

*"Awake, shake dreams from your hair my pretty child my sweet one"*
Jim Morrison, *An American Prayer*

There is a click in the darkness, a tiny flame, then the air is heavy
with psychedelic poison.

Her spine shivers.

He is here again, with his deadly smile and his soft drawl.

It all started with him. Subtle rebellions. The first shiver of sex,
swirling around his hips. A fascination for danger without the
consequences.

She always marvels at how his beauty hangs effortlessly from
his cheekbones. He tells her tall tales of all things forbidden in
smooth whispers. She feigns shock which makes him laugh.
Never for a moment does she forget that this is a seduction.

One night, she'll let his charm win over her cowardice. She always
assumed she'd never be his type, then realised there's no point
in second guessing someone so impulsive. Sometimes he sings,
honey dripping down sandpaper and she is helpless. He smells
like the heady decadence of graveyard flowers. He always asks for
whiskey. She can hear it filling his veins, sucking the life out of
him. But there's no chance in hell she can refuse those wild eyes.

Every time he strolls back into the ether, keeping his secrets
behind his knowing grin, she feels like she is wiser. Then his
songs come over the white noise radio crackles and she forgets he
is a ghost.

She lives vibrant for the length of those songs and dances with abandon. As if his lingering words have cast a spell she cannot shake off, until time is done with itself.

It was always this way with him.

# Ceremony

*"The future's uncertain and the end is always*
*near, let it roll baby roll"*
Jim Morrison, *Roadhouse Blues*


Head back
arms flinging
hot limbs barely saving
my body from falling
and the ground be shaking
the sky could be howling
and I wouldn't notice.
Just that distinct heavy ecstasy
just the poet and the passion
and nothing else can get through
eyes closed to lies
every cell wide open
raw like a broken melody
this is how I love you

# Pére Lachaise*

*"Death makes angels of us all and gives us wings*
*where we had shoulders smooth as ravens claws"*
Jim Morrison, *An American Prayer*


Sun trickled over the monuments to the old illustrious dead.
Elaborate tombstones trashed with graffiti
from fellow seekers trying for an ounce of dangerous beauty.
He lived life brazen and we couldn't look away.
He went wild without apologising
and we basked and swayed in Bacchanalian ecstasy,
knowing people we have no respect for wouldn't get it.

We played records made before we were born,
because it's not like the bad old days
we can only imagine,
where the devil could strut around shameless in black leather,
claim your daughters with a grin,
confuse your sons with a head flick,
enrage men in suits with dirty descants.

We know who we are because of his
blood howling mangled word wisdom.
Skin still tingling from fire dances.

This horde feels like a family I never have to explain myself to.
All I have are photographs,
but my cells remember,
I was there,
in an inescapable reminder of death

---

*The cemetery in Paris where Jim Morrison is buried.

15

and I was elated.
I was there among strangers
and I knew what they hungered for without asking.
I cried at a poet's grave as if he wrote the words for me alone.
I danced the chaos from my twitching bones
as the evening crept back down the alleyways
and for one night,
I was fearless.

# Brazen

*"Before you slip into unconsciousness,*
*I'd like to have another kiss, another flashing chance at bliss"*
Jim Morrison, *The Crystal Ship*


What's it like to be you?
To throw sex around so shameless?
To traverse the Dionysian stars through dark discordant melodies?
To not give a flying fuck what anybody thinks of you?

You taught me that real wildness begins in the mind.
Real art is raw.
Real life is brutal, beautiful and ridiculous all at once
and if I walk away scarless,
it's because I could have done with being a little more brazen.

It scares me how easily I'd let my principals die
for a chance to go back to 67,
claw my way into bed with you,
spread myself open and let you devour me.
Bite your skin to taste pure soft chaos and stagger home
a happy slut,
drunk on sensual anarchy,
not giving two shits if the world thinks
I'm a spoilt brat for wanting more
more

everything.

# This Song

*"The time to hesitate is through, no time to wallow in the mire"*
Jim Morrison, *Light My Fire*

When it hits you like thunder
because you thought the sky was sleeping
like your lungs have grown wings
when you shake and you shake your limbs
rattle out the rancid rambling you spin on repeat
when you just can't help but devour the delicious beat
the heartbeat of the world
the beat of your own private universe
in perfect time

It belongs to everyone,
but it always feels like it's mine

I want to die dancing to this song
feel that split second sting in my heartstrings
before I hit the ground
with those familiar soothing melodies
inducing resurrection rhapsodies
there's no end to it
just press play over and over
I want this crescendo tattooed on my bones
I want to die dancing to this song

It won't be a tragedy
it will be sublime

Because I don't care
when every strand of my hair down to the tips of my toes
basks in the audio glory of my ego's death throes

When you shake and howl and fling your failures
into evanescent spirals
that make the cosmos envious

When it hits your spine and you shudder
hits you like love
the kind of love that lingers after a thousand repeats
when it hits you like love and you shudder
like tomorrow doesn't matter
like nothing lasts forever
but this rhythm never falters never fails
to lift me out of craving and aversion and let balance prevail

Never fails when life tries its nastiest tricks to break me
this is my warrior dance
come at me with all you've got
take me
I am ruthless and raw
floating on forevers and I can only get higher
*come on baby light my fire*
*no time to wallow*
I swallow every note whole and my soul sings

When it hits you and ripples out to the edge
and you want nothing more than to fall
this is what we live for

I want to die dancing to this song
because even though it belongs to everyone
it always feels like it's mine

I want to die a second after the cymbals clash
and it won't be a tragedy
it will be sublime.

# Rebel Soul

*"Have you forgotten the keys to the kingdom? Have you been born yet and are you alive?"*
Jim Morrison, *An American Prayer*

In the cadence of every cell of me,
his poetry, in all its decadent flawed glory,
tangled in reams of bloodied satin sheets
whispering words to be murdered by
in this passion play turned tragic.

He's always sailing on a thin raft
into a strange forever time
at the back of my dreams,
centre stage in a playground of angels and whores,
no one to see him home as he stumbles,
because scapegoats should never be close enough to touch.
Always dancing with death on a back alley tight rope,
howling his name into the dark like a dare,
calling all the wild red headed girls,
desperate for his gentle ruthlessness.
Naked, they fall down into the starry deserts of him
with scars to tell their future by.

He painted over my fears in deadly blues,
sweetened the adolescent spite.
He lied to me softly so I could sleep at night,
with sermon songs,
ostentatious fire.

And it was driving too fast down a drug fuelled highway,
straight into the seediest dive in the darkest alley

to a town I never knew the name of,
because I told the stranger I got in with, to just keep driving,
to the apocalyptic party at the end of all this ugliness
and he smiled wickedly as he named my fear,
handed me my medicine,
turned up the discord until I sweated out all my shame,
dancing on top of his burnt out car,
screaming myself into being.

It must have been like Ancient Greece resurrected,
reduced to a face on my wall,
as kids hang off Parisian balconies drunk on ideas.

We all wonder if you were ever real,
or if you were just so beautiful and barbaric,
we had to invent you.

You burn me up every time even now,
dissolve delusions,
bury me in your bright wise hedonistic nightmares.
I'm never scared because we are dying,
always dying in the slowest cruelest way.
Nothing stalls the sting like your rebel soul fist-kisses,
sliding over my shivering heart like a lover,
hurling me back together into a new shape.

Cold with the sweat of a lunatic god,
he stripped all my disguises down to the bone,
so now I always aim my passion higher than my terror,
with that voice coiled around my skin.

He blows up the stale world with a heavy grinning sigh.

He told them all the lies were true
and they believed him.

# When the Music's Over

She played me my first Doors album.
I was ready, but too young in my awkward bones
for that raw beast of music,
those sensual whispering howls
calling for true oneness.
*Light My Fire* changed my life
in her flat with the bedroom wall she'd painted scarlet red,
to cover her cryptic premonition of her own death,
an assault on her heart.
That's the gift of bands like that,
they make you a little less afraid of your own darkness
as you stare it in the face and dance with it.

"You got me into all my best music"
I told her across the gulf between the chair and the hospital bed,
wanting to hide any finality, but still tell her the truth.
You gave me so much and I'd give it all back if you could stay.

She smiled through her morphine haze,
her arguments with angels
and I knew we both felt it,
our hearts opening with a torrent of pure love,
at the same time subtle like a feather gliding down a river.
The wordless moment where our spirits met,
touched the endless rhythm of the cosmos.

Our last gig was the tribute band,
it was packed but still felt like our secret.
We agreed you could tell he loved the man he was imitating,
you can't fake it with energy that potent.

Every time I dance to them now I feel her there,
the protest against living quietly,
thrumming behind every heartbeat.

# Waves

*For Lisa*

# Waves

My breath stopped.

Split-second-heart-beat-skips.

Excitement filled the silence,
as wave met board
in one of those Point Break "Cowabunga" moments
and I was away,
riding my tired mind straight into my inner child.

I glided, swan-like, onto shore
landing face to face with a dog.
I said "Hi",
he didn't reply,
he's a dog.
But if he could have talked he would have said
"Dude, great wave-riding"
Fact!
So what if it's only a body board,
it's not about technique.
Surfers may have glared the way high school girls in movies
mortify bespeckled geeks but,
in those ten seconds of cool precision,
I was mentally fuck-you-ing every P.E. teacher who ever said
"Lorna lacks basic hand-eye co-ordination."

That holiday was about us
finding secret seal cubs in the harbour dark,
filling our salt-dry cheeks with jam and cream,
tangled wind-beaten sea hair full of damp sand.

It was about courage,
however clumsy.
That Incubus song,
"And in this moment I am happy."
Horizon-gazing daydreams about the perfect summer romance,
I sat watching fragments of pink sunset dance on crest tips.

Even with my eyes shut in the shower I saw waves
and for once I didn't care that he wasn't there,
that my happiness wasn't intricately tied up in his smiles,
forever pushing me out,
pulling me under.

We turned up with nowhere to sleep,
the wind smacking against the phone box like a warning,
but as soon as I saw that Jim Morrison poster,
I knew everything was going to be fine.

We didn't get depressed by tacky seaside arcades,
we got stuck in to 2p machines and catching plastic ducks.
I watched you doing handstands in the sea foam
like a miniature mermaid who just got legs.
We left with moments we didn't need to confirm with words,
just waves.

Those waves we rode shameless and brave,
escape from minimum wage rat race,
back to the wild nature that made us.

We haven't spoken in years,
I think I'd feel awkward now.
You will always be the one who was there when it started,
the slow derailing of all my certainty.

You were drunk and flirting with those two guys
who were making me nervous just for being there
when I got the frantic phone call.

"Your sister's heart's not working properly"

Split-second-heart-beat-skip.

Silence.

Waves.

# Dandelion

1

The corridor seems to get longer with each trip.
It seems cruel when there is suddenly no time.
Yet my steps still slow,
less desperate to reach the end,
because we have been told by three doctors now,
that despite all our disbelief and clinging hope,
she is not coming home from this windowless ward.

I don't make it in time for her last breath,
somewhere under the shock is relief.

She looks peaceful now the machines have stopped blaring,
now nurses have stopped darting in during precious moments.

I kiss her cheek and wish her luck.
I am there in the room,
split open from a clean axe swing,
while my numb heart bursts
in a wasteland with no weather.

Staggering outside I feel unnerved that the sun is blazing,
gasping out alien sounds as birds sing, oblivious.
I pluck a dandelion,
blasting its soft seeds onto an uncertain breeze
and it's all so fragile I can't stand it.

2

The crack in the ceiling of her flat
is more prominent now the room is empty.
We put her life in boxes,
take objects that hold no meaning for us
to charity shops in a shopping trolley.
We sweep bare floorboards and close the window.
We leave for the last time.
No more Sunday roasts she has yet to cook
when we arrive with growling stomachs.


3

"Nothing could be done"
I say to friends who haven't seen her for years.
I believe it when I tell them I'm fine,
a primitive part of my brain accepting the natural order.

It's later the wrecking ball finds me.
When my feet finally landed and kept sinking,
I understood why some people just jump.

At my worst I didn't know how to fill the next hour
with anything resembling contentment.
Now I can flick through photo albums,
tolerate patiently this nameless fear
tugging at my nerve endings.

Walk down a hospital corridor without feeling cheated.

# Hospital

*For Milo and Kim*

1

I had a hunch you were on your way. So I steeled myself to walk into
that hospital, after all this time. Fear crashing down with full force, I
said sheepishly to the receptionist,
"I think my friend's having a baby here right now."
She directed me to the next building. One where I'd never lost
anyone. I was relieved. There was space.

I sat with your future grandparents and waited. Half excited, half
nervous. Full of something there's no words for. Opposite us I
could see the ward where she died and with her, my naive belief in
everything staying the same. I couldn't give the feeling a name. I just
remember contradictions.

I hate hospitals.
Thank God for hospitals.
Life always carries on.
Thank God we die,
so it means something.

I held you an hour after you were born,
the newest person I've ever met.

The kind of vulnerability I could stand, surrounded by bright white
walls and busy nurses. I felt that weird guilt that I had no right to
be there with someone else's family, borrowing love. Shaking with
unexpected sadness even as you filled my arms, I swallowed down a
sob and focused on the moment.

"Well that's that then", your mum said with her typical non-chalant determination. Like she hadn't just been in labour for twenty-four hours. I laughed, emboldened by the symbology of you. There's nowhere to go but forward and that's that.


2


You love pegs. Sure those bright noisy plastic toys entice you for awhile, but you always go back to the pegs and cupboards. Taking stuff out and staring at it intently, putting it back in then taking it out again. It never stops being funny.

Buddha was right about immediate needs and simple wants. There is only the present moment that can do you any good, surrender.

I never appreciated the juvenile fun of just bashing things. We shout babble into plastic pots like we're an intergenerational post-modern punk band. My elastic faces get giggles from you that crack me up, an antidote to the brutal invasion of grief.

I envy your fearlessness. I should learn from it and jump in with both feet finally. Because it helped, you coming along, new and vital.

I'm actually quite good at this. I've no broody aspirations. I can give it my all because I can give you back. I never quite shake that old anxiety. What if I break you? We're all so fragile.

Since my howling in a hospital corridor, cells still raw with it, I can't always stand the pressure of love or the hazy gap that it leaves behind. But that's no excuse is it? I will be braver now.

She was good with kids. Always the cool Auntie figure,
creasing impressionable foreheads with pensive questioning.
In the end, they would believe her, because she told the truth.

"I can make it rain, watch"

and the heavens would always open.

# You Sent Me Horses

It started with two Shetlands in a field in Somerset.
I realised that to remind me you were still here,
all wild kind and subtle,
you had sent me horses.

For the heavy void filling my skull,
you sent me a boisterous black gelding
and two patient mares,
whose loyalties I charmed with carrots
between doctor's appointments.
You led me to a sanctuary,
where like me,
they'd had too much go on in too short a time,
they needed some comfort and safety.

Now,
the time I wasted too terrified to leave the house,
too terrified to stay,
is spent with mud caked around my boots,
as I shovel muck and distribute hay
and I've never been happier.
Sharing silence with the subjects of
all those Grecian Myths and Celtic Legends made flesh,
Pegasus, Shadowfax, Bucephalus.

Time,
which stretched out in endless reminders of loss,
can be filled with nothing more than the nuzzling of a soft nose
to make life seem worth the danger.
The spotting of robins in the corner of a stable,
the rare sight for these city eyes

of a landscape full of trees and hills,
sunsets,
I'd missed those.

Now I'm learning to steer my way into chaos,
the exhilaration of speed on the back of a gentle beast
that gives away their power if you're kind and patient,
this is how the mind is sometimes and how you must teach it.

I'm slow and clumsy,
but they can tell I mean well
as we navigate untrustworthy obstacles together.
Puddles,
sudden noises,
troublesome strangers.
I've been scared of these tiny traumas too.
A constant thought that sticks like tar,
a song on the radio with no warning,
trembling bones and squeezed-out lungs
in an Airbnb bathroom I should not be in,
not in a state like this.
The persistent prey-like drive for flight,
"Run. You're not safe"

I tried to be kind to the jolting jerking
animal that replaced me,
foaming at the mouth with fear, pulling at reins made of air,
but it was too strong for me.
Horses have a sturdier kind of fragility.
Death is scratching at the heels of everything,
but at least if you ride, your feet are off the ground.

With them, I see how I'm like them,
half wild, half tame,

half in this world, half in yours,
half here, beneath my palm,
breathing long and deep,
half the stuff of legend charging into battle.
I was half of myself,
now I am almost a Centaur,
daring to hold my ground,
flare my nostrils with defiance.

I'm always putting my forehead against theirs
as we stand completely still.
I know they know what I'm thinking,
this is how it feels to be peace-full.

You sent me those horses
we always meant to ride together but never did.
One day I'll soar over this pit of regret
as I gallop into the unknown,
making hoof prints big enough to leave an old life in,
breathless,
terrified,
smiling,
gone.

# Valentine's Day

I am baby-sitting in the Scottish Borders.
Warm and floppy-limbed from the bath,
I pull on layers and brave the cold to check my charges.

The night is crisp with winter,
the stars just showing off.
You don't get constellations like this in Birmingham.

The air smells of hay.
I step silently in between the boys and for a second,
it feels like we are all looking up at the moon entranced,
not a thought in our heads.
"Who needs a man when I've got you two gorgeous beasts?"
One answers me with a curious frisk right in my face,
he's such a flirt.
The other is more guarded,
but I can tell he's getting used to my bumbling presence,
enjoying my celery-filled pockets.
It means something that I stand between them
feeling contentment and sadness at the same time.
One had it easy and is all friendly curiosity and hand licks,
the other is a handful to those who don't know
they're looking at ingrained fear.

The yard feels pleasantly eerie in the dark.
Somewhere across the fields of trees planted in straight lines,
harbouring the kinds of mushrooms you only see in fairy tales,
an owl hoots while the rescue pigs sleep.

I saw my first live badger here
while I was on horse-back.

We both froze and stared as it ambled by
on its nocturnal adventures, unfazed.

I never knew hares were so golden,
that buzzards were so big,
that deer could run so fast on legs so spindly.

She would have loved it here,
my second home.
The quiet,
the subtle way nature just gets on with itself,
the rubbing of soft noses against lonely skin.

It hurts a little less to miss her
in a place with so many stars.

# Sunflowers

I've kept that last bottle of perfume
you always got me for Christmas for years now.
I know I should just give in
to the extravagance of using it every day.
Why not?
Those special occasions I save perfume for
are sporadic and rarely that special in the end.
Why shouldn't I feel like that divine nature goddess
I've been channelling in yoga classes all the time?
Life's too short for hanging back.

I have other gifts from you that will last after me,
but there's something so engulfing
then fleeting about the realm of scent.

I think I'm scared of how I'll feel
when it finally runs out.
Once it's gone it's gone.
I've had enough of that neutral viciousness to last me.

I can't remember your smell anymore.

# Red Sea

The blissful silence of swimming at sunrise,
without a hint of cold in the sticky air
and the waves too lazy to try.
Where you can feel rather than hear
the rush of blood through a serene heart,
cradled in a land that's never seen snow.

The weightless sensation of hovering between land and ocean,
diving into the divide to watch another world
gliding to its own rhythm.
The *Little Mermaid* moment I've craved since I was eight.

The breath-stealing moment of seeing a shooting star
bounce off the earth's curve in the pitch-black night.
I kept that moment to myself.

After we got so stoned we couldn't stop laughing,
we went night swimming
to cool our scorching bodies,
 "Careful in there, there's creatures that will sting you"
So we behaved ourselves,
but part of me wanted to just dive in and drift away.

This is where I remember seeing you happy,
sand between your toes,
calm in every face crease,
like you were home.
This complete love beyond words for life itself.

This is where I let my memory go
when I can't find you.
There you are,
under the thatched veranda of your beach shack,
face covered by cheap sunglasses,
swatting at flies for daring to interrupt you
pretending to read,
sipping mint tea,
sizing up the locals,
lapping up the light and the clear blue everything,
Queen of the desert.

# Altar

She bought it online on a whim,
the one bulky item I insisted on keeping.
A wooden table,
with delicate mosaic tiles encased under glass.

I've filled it full of rocks from far away beaches,
pigeon feathers tied up with kestrels,
no less beautiful for being grey.
Statues of Aphrodite, Thoth and Bast,
ready to be consulted on matters of cosmic importance.

Object by object I add to her temple.
My crystals,
my essentials oils,
my witching tools,
my "hippie nonsense"
I keep this space sacred.
Remember all she taught me about bigger picture love,
the sound of the universe throbbing in my heart.

There's no superstition in this ritual,
it makes perfect sense to me,
keeping the mind out of what it can't comprehend.
This absolute present moment,
this honouring of ancient nature,
among the thick grey carpet and whirring radiator.

This temple gleams with all the forest floors colour,
takes me out of time into an older world,
when talismans were found in the dirt rather than scrolled down
and we knew how to respect death.

A piece of coral she found in the desert in Egypt,
riding her camel Charlie Brown while everyone else was napping,
a non descript stone I plucked
from the Fairy Pools on the Isle of Skye,
after asking permission.
A note she wrote for me in a women's workshop,
"I wish you true friendship, true love, prosperity"

These are the treasures you can throw in when I burn.
The rest of the house only spews her absence back at me,
tells you nothing about our shared passions.
The rest of the house can gather dust
and go to hell.

# Tiny Victories

I know what love is now.
What's worth the gut-howling.

I've become one of those people who stop mid power-walk
to stare at trees and bask in birdsong.
I can cry with joy at the sight of a starling pecking at breadcrumbs.

I've learned to wash up singing to the radio again.

I'm finding better ways to waste the day.

Wounds take time to sink in and find their place
before you can stop crying at bus stops.

I'm starting to lean into my hope at last,
hiding at the corners of my mouth saying
"smile, it's alright, the worst is over"

There's much to be said for subtle rebellions,
tiny victories.

The cost of being achingly human,
now your heart has returned to stardust.

# Instructions for Grief

Grief is something unspeakable.
There are no satisfying words for its catastrophes.
But try to find some that do it justice,
so its power is pliable.

Grief will bring you to your knees.
Let it.
Let yourself fall.

Grief will give you a generous dose of useless guilt.
Get rid of it,
however long it takes,
it has nothing to teach you.

Grief will tear you open.
Let it.
Let it rip you up in the cruellest ways,
leave your wounds open for time to close,
show your scars.

Grief will change you forever,
yet almost everything else will be the same.
Make peace with these contradictions.
Nothing will ever be black and white again,
it never was.
Learn to love your brain full of barbed wire,
your belly full of black-holes.

Edges will smooth,
emptiness will fill itself with is-ness.

Grief is messy.
Let it be.
You will find its grit under your fingernails
at the most inappropriate moments,
but you will be clean again.

Grief will make you think too much
eat too little
sleep sporadically
if at all
feel in every cell that the world is not safe anymore.

It's never been safe.

Smother your fear with patience,
try and remember you're worth taking care of.

Grief will break you,
Let it.
Let your heart shatter,
see each piece clearly.
What's so wrong with a few cracks?
*"That's how the light gets in."*

Grief will stop you.
Let it for a while,
then relearn perpetual motion.

Grief is never over,
there is more to come,
but you need not lock the door,
sharpen your sword and wait for the invasion,
just leave a place at the table and carry on.

Grief is perfectly normal,
it inevitably happens to everyone,
but your grief is yours alone.

Your grief, my grief, their grief.
Say it until it's just another term in a self-help book,
just a word that means nothing.

Say it for what it really means,
the end of someone your love couldn't save.
It doesn't mean your love is useless,
it's the reason everything will be okay.

Sit beside your sadness and make it comfortable,
so life can happen to you again,
in all its beautiful awful and fleeting wonder.

# Tide

I know why the sea makes sense to me now.
There's no plan,
just lows and highs
that steal my footsteps.

As the years went by,
you made your world smaller.
There are fewer photos of your face.
But I knew when you got in your rickety white van
on another unplanned adventure,
eventually I'd see a picture of your bare sandy feet.
It became a tradition.
"Here I am"

Rooted on a shore somewhere between
the solid and the infinite,
one always getting worn down by the other.

You'll never make another footprint,
the sea has them all now.
the trails of all your escapes.

When I walk the shoreline,
those waves playing around my feet as they sink down,
but never so deep that I can't keep going,
I realise,
I'm bigger than the trap I've locked myself in,
deeper than the cracks I've carved into my skin,
built to withstand endless hits and retreats.
I won't drown just for stepping a little lighter,
trusting the pull of an unpredictable tide.

I'll wash up somewhere that looks like love,
take photos of my feet and remember
"Here I am"

Slowly but surely,
the sea will have her way,
whispering that everything that happens in you
happens in the universe too
and it can unravel without dropping a stitch,
missing a beat,
thinking it through and if everyday
as the sun rises,
the world learns how to begin again,
so can you.

Split-second-heart-beat-skip.

Silence.

Waves.

# Sacred

*"The truth about ourselves is stored in our body and although we can repress it, we can never alter it. Our intellect can be deceived, our feelings manipulated, but someday our body will present its bill, and will accept no compromises or excuses and it will not stop tormenting us until we stop evading the truth."*
Alice Miller

# Tight

I let him ruin me
with my own illusion of unworthiness,
not enough-ness.
I didn't say no,
though my body changed my mind about yes,
but I just carried on getting it over with.
It never forgave me for giving in,
even as I second guessed.
It tried to tell me in many ways of its
angry disappointed otherness

        disconnect

but I ignored it,
so it had to destroy me.

I'm not making it up,
this solid coiled-up feeling.
I feel it in every cell of my body,
*my* body.
I feel it despite the world's lies,
the rolling eyes,
the confused stare,
the embarrassed silence that comes with talking about
"Down there"

But the fact is,
it's everywhere,
all the time,
we carry it with us.
All this weight we are expected to take.

We feel it,
we are tired of it,
we are not making it up.

Just because it doesn't fit with the performance or the taboo,
just because it's a little bit awkward for you.
What goes on in the bedroom
isn't a whole other plain of existence
you only get to play on if you're "normal."
We are not "normal",
another chain to weigh ourselves down.
But we are not broken.
We are perfectly flawed for being real,
for feeling it in our bodies,
our bodies,
and thriving all the same.

You are making us up
and we are done with illusions.
We want to fall into bed with the truth,
the flawless truth,
as we make ourselves.

*Vaginismus is a psychosomatic/psychosexual condition I had for
over twenty years, estimated to affect two in every thousand women
and making vaginal penetration of any kind painful and often
impossible.*
www.thevaginismusnetwork.com

# Sacred

Nobody taught me you were sacred.
Each river having the right to flow unhindered,
each curve untouchable unless invited.
I didn't have words for this untapped power
hemmed in by mistrust,
brimming under the surface
seemingly calm,
destined to unleash chaos without warning
so it could thrive, finally.
That you have the right to be nurtured without negligence,
asked permission.

Nobody taught me what you were trying to tell me.
This is the worst thing we do to each other,
nobody telling anybody that everybody is worthy.

I was too green though I was grown,
a sapling inching tentatively towards a sun
you've been scorched by,
but you send me rain though I call it a storm,
so I'm sorry.
For tethering you to the pressure of a world
that ignores your primal pain,
your subtle abundant perseverance,
knocking softly patiently waiting,
ready to bloom,
gently opened
then sated.

Nobody teaches us the truth of ourselves,
nobody told me you were sacred.

# Lonely Strokes

When I was young,
I used to masturbate on the sofa in the middle of the day.

I don't know what compelled me to want to get caught,
didn't have the words for it.
I just knew the gifts of my body were not for display,
not to be tentatively discussed in the illusion of privacy,
not deemed worthy of a mention in Sex Education.
Something I should feel guilty for and cease.

Now I know it was a plea to be seen.
My desire vital, alive, natural,
despite averted eyes and coy subject changes and silence
and silence and silence.

It was longing,
screaming to connect these distant enquiries
to a body I couldn't escape,
or persuade anyone to touch,
that was not my enemy.

Silence was the enemy.
Their pretending they hadn't seen and walking out the room,
when I would rather have been berated.
All these sharp contradictions packed into my sacred cave,
to keep it tame and silent and dull.

My chalice of creation that I never ventured into,
but lay out as a sacrifice to the unworthy.

If I could go back to that moment,
where I spread myself open out of desperation,
I would have set the teeth of my cunt on his cowardice,
his indifferent invasion,
to make him see me.

I know every inch of it now,
of her.
I can clamp her shut at will,
I can open her up and devour the world's toxicity,
swallow it into the void of me and birth something new,
this scares you and it makes me brave.

I can create private pleasures,
or announce them proudly,
no more lonely strokes,
every slick exploration an act of revelation.

I have caught fire finally,
singeing all who look,
but don't dare to see me
in my splendour.

# Drawn from Life

I am not myself.
I am the figure.
All jagged angles and constant proportions.

I am made of circles and triangles,
lines and curves.
Making negative space with my jutting elbows,
filling the air with straightness.

They all have a different version of the picture
the world has drawn on me.
The girls have shiny black shoes and kind smiles,
the boys don't snigger or look at the floor,
I am a study to be taken seriously.

I am not paraded,
posed to perfection,
arranged for maximum allure.
There are no lies,
only the truth of the body as it is.
The only rule,
the rule of thumb.

I am graphite and charcoal and smudges.
The outline of someone who could be anyone.
Who doesn't need words quirks or tricks
to pull the eye.

I am described as tall with high cheekbones,
interesting hands.
I did not know these things about myself.

I am measured in pencils,
not marked for the quality of my mask.

I am fibula, knuckle joint, clavicle.
I am rubbed out and restarted but remain unfinished.

Sometimes they move their heads
from the easels to me and back in unison.
That's the only perfection here.

I never would have dared this sensual exposure
before tragedy cracked me open and made a new skin.

One that sees how shyness wastes too much time,
losing paint with every brushstroke.

The precise beauty of dissection.

The unexpected liberation of being looked at,
but not seen.

# Wild Swim

1

The sludge will try to suck me down.
My arms will tangle in those swaying tendrils.
But the sun is blazing a thousand diamonds
and the still clear blue is begging me.
I am alone in the subtle crackles of nature's silence.
My body wants to be new again.
To float and be stroked by the world as it was
before limbs came along to move it.
I strip with a knowing grin,
feeling like of a siren of the loch
and the swans can watch if they want to.
I will welcome the cool caressing love the water gives me freely.
I breathe out and dip a tentative foot,
I'm going in.


2

I don't know the names of most of them,
Latin or common,
I bet the bees don't even bother with some,
too small and simple smelling.

But when I open the bag I have filled,
breathe in the heady sensuality
of their combined perfume,
when I sprinkle them over the water,
candles burning,
rose quartz crystals gleaming,

I feel like Cleopatra about to descend into her
gold plated bath of asses milk,
feel this otherwise forgettable day becoming one to cherish.

I swirl nature's rainbow around my body with my fingers.
This is the nearest I'll get to goddess-hood,
to stumbling through the darkest part of the forest
into the sumptuous kingdom of The Fae.

I may be in a pokey bathroom with blackened tiles,
in what was once the most notorious council estate in the area,
but for tonight I am a queen
and to tell the truth,
I could stay until my skin wrinkles off my body,
adorned with purple buddleia, wild jasmine, dog rose,
blending with the petals,
until I dissolve.

# Soul Sisters

*For the Coven*

This starlit sky is our temple,
this crackling fire a reminder
that we are light made flesh,
as the moon kisses our skin and we dance.
Like our sisters did before us in the ancient days,
sweating out the carnage,
offering the darkness our victorious howls,
wearing our scars as jewels that shine like foxes eyes.
In a circle round a tree stump as old as time,
we remake the world beautiful with our dexterous hands,
as we breathe ourselves back into peace with words.
We are wounded warriors,
always ready for battle,
but never forgetting our time is better spent talking to trees,
painting birds wings on birch bark,
gifting each other with nature's bounty.
Casting our fortunes by the cosmos,
the weight of our fears become footprints on the shore,
for the tide to roll away at our command.
Then we wash ourselves soul pure,
until we glow silver.
We are a many limbed ubiquitous goddess,
laughing at petty wars,
armed with spider webs and witches spells.
We have eaten the hearts of our would-be destroyers
and live despite the poison,
we have no intention of behaving ourselves.

# V is for Vagina

When I'm feeling fun,
need to keep it casual,
I call it my fanny.
It makes me feel safe and a bit cheeky all at once.
In those everyday conversations,
to call it something more serious can feel loaded,
there's enough pressure on that place already.

Yes, another empowered
Viva Vagina poem
and there should be more,
many more.
There's enough silent vaginas,
so the ones who can talk should shout loud.
(I know if I'm being woke and inclusive I should call it my vulva,
but it just doesn't have the same poetic syntax as vagina,
this is my choice and we should all respect that.)

When I'm horny,
it's my pussy.
Problematic pornography aside,
when that word is whispered in my ear by a lover
with the words,
"I'm going to fuck your beautiful..." before it
and I believe him,
it's the sexiest word I've ever heard
and I'm wet willing and waiting,
for the next man who can say pussy and mean it.

When I'm feeling rebellious and political,
I call it my cunt.
It shouldn't be that big a deal this day and age,
a generic word for a body part.
Left elbow, toe, nipple, cunt.
Cunt.
I like the way it sounds in my mouth,
no nonsense,
packs a resonating punch.

Nothing shocks me about her anymore.
She is a she,
this part of me,
for all that life has tried to steal her from me,
she's mine.
She was tangled up tight for a long time,
her first visitor was indifferent to her heart and mind
and she cried and battened down the hatches,
so I could just move on,
blot out the psychological bleeding,
for years and years,
until she started screaming,
so now I let her speak,
because I like being alive.

My favourite word for her is yoni,
Sanskrit for sacred cave, earliest abode, dwelling place
and other gorgeous primordial words of the earth,
to be passed on to soul sisters as we dance naked under moonlight.
All she's ever wanted is for her power to be acknowledged,
but I had to teach her this power in secret,
as we fell down internet rabbit holes
and tried to deconstruct shame.
Together we made our own language,

because if there's one thing the world
doesn't want to talk about it's vaginas,
especially when they don't do what they were paid to do.
She has passed her initiation finally and wants to celebrate,
she fucking deserves it,
along with a yacht and a castle and all the ice cream she can eat,
because she's a queen.
If you want her to bestow her generous bounty,
you bow and play nice.

Woe betide those who don't respect all she can do.
Wage war,
defuse bombs,
dance the tango,
survive on barely nothing,
take you to heaven and back,
save the planet,
because when you heal the womb you heal the world,
fact.

She is magic and wondrous and yours is too,
so next time she calls you
pick up the phone and tell her you love her too.
No one else can do this for you
and if you don't she will die,
or she will kill you,
or the world will take her from you and turn her against you,
trust me,
take back her power so she's not erased from the alphabet,
spread your two fingers and raise them proudly,
V is for Vagina
and she will be heard.

# A Virgins Guide to Hiring an Escort

*For D*

# This is a Love Story

See her in her jasmine scented Airbnb, pacing in anticipation. Her
friend's gift of a flowery dressing grown billowing with every sharp
direction change.

She is more ugly sister or witch than princess, all hard jaw, awkward
limbs and repressed rage. Right up until the moment she opens the
door to let the stranger in, you would think her a girl still, a
shivering mass of naïve worry. Not at all prepared for the longed for
yet unknown terrain of sensuality. But as she hesitantly welcomes in
this new adventure, who offers a kiss on each cheek, see her catch up
to herself. A creature of imploding now blooming. Watch her
ripening body dance off her script of apologies, all sweaty with
gossamer desire.

Yes your eyes are drawn to him, he's the beautiful one. Not the usual
hulking pride-heavy presence, no wolf teeth barred. Cast him as a
wandering troubadour whose songs spin seduction.
A magician whose robes smell of something intoxicating and
forbidden. A natural temptress.

She knows nothing about him, except the one thing that matters.
When he asks her desire to come out and play, she can say yes, and
no axes will fall, her heart won't be eaten. She will break it on him of
course, and it will feel cruel, but necessary. She doesn't know this yet,
she thinks she can handle the banquet she has ordered.

She says yes.

Afterwards, watch her fall deep into the mattress, shaking with calm
joy. All dragons slain, all mazes gently twisted back into one flow. It's
not magic, this transformation, it's just nature. It looks like nothing

much has changed, but now she can stand tall and run without stumbling, talk desire without stammering, take without begging.

The shameless enchantress awakened in her juicy cunt wants more, so she feasts. He is generous.

Watch her full breath escape and return in sated slumber as he leaves the room, his chapter over though his presence will linger forever. Her story finally starting.

It's not a passive sleep. Watch the monster of shame die with every memory of sweat kiss and hungry suck, now encoded in the bones.

Isn't she glorious? This girl and woman united, finally.

This is a love story.

# I want you to

I want you go down on me for ages.
I want you to tell me exactly how you like you dick sucked
because I want to go to town on it.
I want you to bend me over and go at me and call me a good girl.
I want you to whip me until I'm red raw and call me a bad girl.
I want you to cum in my mouth on my face on my tits,
just cum all over me.

> I want you to kiss me.
> I know it sounds pathetic,
> but I've never really been kissed properly.
> Just kiss me.
> I want you to touch me,
> every inch of my skin.
> Nobody touches me.
> Nobody wants to touch me.

Tell me how to please you.
I know you're here for me but
I crave your approval.
I don't like being in charge.
I want to be safe to be weak.

> Just make me feel desirable, seen,
> loved.
> Just fuck it out of me.
> All this toxic bullshit I've been carrying around
> my whole life goddamn life.
> That's kept me lonely and shame filled and scared.
> Just fuck me.

I want you to fuck me.

# Skin

Fizzing with anxious need,
I clock-watch and breathe tightness.
Beat my raw naivety down with begging
please just give me this,
let it happen,
make it work.

Your effortless sensuality hits me like a wave.
Be careful with me I plead silently.
You don't need to hear it,
you read my body shaking with need,
jittering hands fascinated by the promise of skin.

I kiss you first,
I'm proud of myself.
Suddenly I cease to feel that cold dread.
I'm warm for once,
the warmth of you,
makes me throw it all at you in one go.
I'm too much,
I know,
but it doesn't matter,
you give me all of you anyway.
Reward me for my bravery with teasing expert hands,
laughter, insight, soothing commands.

"Relax.
Tell me.
Touch yourself.
Look at me"

I gave myself a rule that I wouldn't say sorry.
Of course I break it in my eagerness,
but this time,
it's about what pleases me.
You can tell this terrifies me so you take charge.
I think I start to say sorry on purpose.
Utterly seduced by this woman I don't recognise,
but always knew myself to be,
intrigued by how quickly she's unleashed with a playful slap,
"Stop apologising"
It's never felt so good to be this infuriating.

All I needed was permission,
to know it's not something I can do wrong.
It's easy in this electric blissful now,
bodies entwined without the cringe-worthy clichés
or posturing angles.
You're a gentle animal,
the facilitator for my dormant power,
unearthed in bumbling acts of revelation,
I am allowed,
invited.
I am desired,
desiring.

My desire has a purpose that isn't setting me up to fall,
sated instead of doused down,
or bitterly resented for existing at all.
I don't even care who can hear my moans through the wall,
devour me.
down to the last shred of loneliness that was killing me slowly,
I surrender.

Bold in my urge to relinquish control,
my hips take on the swagger of a woman free of fear
to be touched, kissed, fucked, seen.
I am done with deprivation
because I was drowning.
I felt no shame in asking you to teach me to swim.
It wasn't about something new,
it was about remembering.
Kick back, dive in, trust your lungs.
Run exploratory fingers over inviting lips,
receive uncomplicated attention,
release the world's weight.

Breath in ear,
neck shiver,
that spot on my spine that jolts me right there,
sweat salt hands in hair don't stop.

It kills me that it will have to stop.

Hearts dance exploding implode.
I've broken into sweet pieces of chaos
that find their way back together without parasitic glue.
Gold is the only worthy element to reforge me anew,
thank you.

You teach me to be proud of this natural creature.
How to be kind to her instead of pulling her apart
as you pull her pain apart gently,
gentle animal.
I'm pulled up into thudding chest,
held in time-stretching oblivion.

I get it now.
Forgive all the time I wasted
thinking I knew nothing.
It's mine now.
The whole world of desire reclaimed.

I don't sleep a wink,
the sound of another's breath beside me,
skin lazily grazing skin,
too overwhelming.
Anyone who would begrudge me this,
never felt what it's like to be in this body,
once frozen and enraged,
now on fire with its own freedom.
You helped me know myself more stranger-lover,
than anyone who knew me who threw me
by supposedly knowing better.
Now I know better.
that it's how I feel first,
no one else's fucking business how I quench my thirst,
after so long wandering in the hinterland of useless want.

You were everything I needed
without feeling a fool to need.
You were worth every penny.

# Feast

I was not prepared for the feast of you.
So long starving,
begging for scraps,
to suddenly be so full.
Invited to have my fill
of the gift of your body,
the sweet tang of your sweat,
the soft ceasing of thought,
as your teeth gently bit my lip
and brought me to life.

It took me endless awkward seconds to answer you,
this throat full of thorns
finally untangling,
for someone willing to wrap my vines around and flourish.
How can it happen so quickly?
This much luck,
to flush out all that stinging nettle hunger
in a heartbeat.

I bury all my broken down hope in your arms
and wake up reborn.
You have slain me and I shimmer
in the fire of desolation.

Blissfully ignorant of that unconscious part of me
that is already mourning,
knowing this will be over before I am ready.

# Bite

It's how I know it was real,
along with that gorgeous twinge in my cells when I remember.
Red indents in my pale skin tell
how I was ripe for devouring,
worthy of being feasted on.

It makes me feel strong
to have been so deliciously wounded.
Excites me that the evidence lingers
and I can keep it secret,
or display it proudly,
no explanation necessary.
You could tell from my smile alone,
how I have been given to and taken all at once.

See outside of this room,
I am no one,
instantly forgettable.
In here,
proudly sticking out my bare arse
because you insist you love curves,
I am your cheap slut goddess
every time whip thrashes skin.

With each stroke I understand how I'm the one in control,
as I moan and squirm into and away from
those exquisite little pleasure pains,
cosmic desire coursing through my veins and fuck,
it's heaven.

Unlike the wolves outside,
who I would never stoop to,
you will not draw blood from me.
Only adrenalin filled aftershocks that thrill me for days,
so potent I forget my name.
There's only room for yours on my good little sub tongue,
Master,
Stranger.

When the marks fade I'm disappointed,
deprived of the last physical trace of you,
because I'm still burning,
desperate to gorge on you again
and who would blame me,
if they ever felt their flesh shudder under your mouth?
Ecstatically happy to worship and be worshipped accordingly.

You introduced me to this salacious lover
I always wanted to meet,
so I could pull her out of my head and share her.

To lie back and just take all you have to offer,
because I am the gift.

I never thought I'd be so naturally submissive.
Any other scenario I wouldn't stand for it,
the relinquishing of power.
But here in this suspended reality,
paid for by the hour,
this woman who until tonight was still a shivering girl,
blushing and stuttering,
is yours to pin down
and mark as your own.

# Leda*

For a moment I am Leda,
both afraid and in awe.
Knowing instinctively,
this one is not the same as the others,
all preening and aloof
like a dressing room full of lazy divas,
this one is a hunter.

I was not prepared as I turned the corner,
sun shimmering diamonds on the lake,
to see such a legion of brightness,
a whiteness of swans.
It feels other-worldy,
like I have somehow shrunk
and I'm speechless.
Ironically mute.
It's pure mythology
and my epic heart is racing into metaphors.

This one is not intimidated,
instead of hiss there is silence,
surety as he steps towards me fearlessly.
Throwing the food doesn't deter him,
he is coming for me,
for the whole offering.

---

*Leda was the mother of Helen of Troy and was seduced by
Zeus in the guise of a swan.

It's because I'm still feathered with the memory of you,
that I see the potential for sensuality everywhere.
Still feel your weight encasing me
in pounding thoughtless joy.
It's because of your whispers in my ear,
your bite marks still red on my shoulder,
that I find this animal's advance intriguing.

Before I would have appeased,
given in.
Now,
I puff my chest out and hold my ground,
unwavering will in my bones,
feeling taller somehow.

I step forward and hold space,
so he knows I'm not to be taken lightly.

This Leda is not to be trifled with,
seduced by something shiny as if it's harmless.
You are no posturing god,
your yielding masculinity is beautiful.
The swan is just a swan,
yet all three of us radiate power in our own ways.

I advance,
heart ablaze,
he backs off,
I stride emboldened,
I am coming for the world.

# George Michael Slow Dance

Despite everything you and I have done together,
the hungry bites,
the soft kisses,
the whip,
the blindfold,
I still don't have the nerve to ask for what I want the most.
It sounds so corny and tame.

I want to slow dance with you to George Michael's 'Father Figure.'

It's not even a kinky thing.
I want us fully clothed,
hips swaying in time,
your arms around my waist,
my face nestled in your neck,
like some Hollywood prom movie
I thought I'd outgrown,
now I finally know how well reality can deliver,
that romance is vapid bullshit.

I don't know why it embarrasses me so much.
Something so casual,
yet so intimate.
It's not the same as what we do in bed.

I know there are better songs to slow dance to,
that the lyrics are problematic for our official arrangement,
my vulnerability,
your mastery,
but nevertheless,
slow dance to George Michael with me.

Because I've never slow danced with a man before.

I want us alone in our own private room,
away from the sleazy gyrating of a dance-floor.

It's somehow more intense
than your tongue on my clit,
my hands tugging at your hair,
we may never get there.
It could be way too expensive
in a subtle heart-ripping way.
I can't really have you
once that loaded song is over,
not to keep anyway.

Never mind,
it's silly really,
I'll probably never ask.

Because when you slow dance to George Michael's 'Father Figure'
there really is no going back.

# Pearl

When I was done with drowning,
let my glinting glass edges
begging for touch despite the warning,
smooth under the flood of you,
I realised I could deep dive after all.
I didn't need to hold my breath,
crush every ounce of power down into my lungs
to keep myself afloat but not thriving.
I could just exhale,
keep unfurling,
rise
and never grasp for another greedy gulp to live.
My sharpness worn down to a palm sized gift
that the hand naturally curls around
and squeezes because it feels like home.

All the myths I'd grinded into my hope,
until it was heavy and I hoarded it crab-like.
As aloof as a gull,
hovering but never landing,
scaled in armour,
afraid to kick out alone
because the sea is cruel unless you turn shark.

I didn't know I would sink into you so utterly,
until I realised I was already there,
waiting between tides,
long before I knew you.

In that liquid evening of the exploration of flesh,
the salvaging of sex,
I remembered,
the wreck of me is still beautiful,
every time the sunlight shimmers
through the kelp,
cuts up the dark
and finds the pearl of me,
the moon of womanhood,
the world under the world.

# Crying at the Orgy

I've learned in the most sublime and vicious way,
that if you starve desire it doesn't die,
it just eats you instead.
So what you force to be small screams to thrive,
makes you run from the one thing that makes you feel alive,
because god forbid anyone should hear your true animal,
howling.

And this is all I can think about in the middle of the orgy.

How all this welcoming slippery freedom
doesn't even come close to the moment you said,
"You're brave" and I believed you.
Then you fucked me,
that's why I hired you,
but you felt like my friend as well as my fantasy,
so I wasn't scared of you like I am now.
Scared when I thought I'd come so far,
earned my sexual liberation.

I don't feel liberated now,
among the pink neon lit limbs and the scent of rose oil,
as strangers grind to sensuous baselines,
with Tesco's own snacks in polystyrene bowls on the sidelines.

Plastic cups with names stickers on,
there I am: 'Lorna.'
I feel like to even pick it up would declare me an imposter.
Because what the fuck am I doing here?
Less than a week after I told my friend,
"I know I said don't worry but it turns out I did fall for him"

But I do feel safe here,
it's curated,
there are rules.
I continued to pay for the chaos to be compartmentalised.
This is the only way I can digest the tangled variables of sex,
which brings a new terror.

All that bravado when I straddled you,
sucked you greedily,
when I kissed you first,
me, the girl who would shut down
even a conversation about sexual intimacy.
Who by our third encounter,
handed you a whip and a blindfold and said,
"Do whatever you want to me"
I thought she was here to stay,
after bursting through the stage door of shame
to make such a grand sensual debut.
She it turns out,
can only be unleashed when she's with you
and right now she's tearing up my shiny new guts,
hating me for making her miss you,
here crying in the middle of the orgy.

"This is just so typical of you", she sneers,
as bodies slap and sweat and oil and saliva mingle
in a cacophony of pleasure moans.
"When will you understand no one is coming to save you?
You have to keep saving yourself, that's what makes people
want you back"

She's right of course.
She was there mocking me when I would whisper "I love you"
into the space between your shoulder blades,

not sure how much I meant it.
How could I know?
Nothing to compare it to.
I just had to let the words out,
in case I never got another moment that warranted them.
That's the trouble with the consistently starved,
we tend to sink our teeth in too deep,
lest our long awaited rewards get snatched away.

But no one, especially not you would blame me,
for ducking out of all this potential and crying at the orgy,
wanting you pointlessly,
surrounded by twenty nine other people there for the literal
taking.

Every cell of me has been re-forged under your mouth
and I'm irrevocably charged to keep gorging,
because there's no putting the toothpaste back in the tube,
or in this case, lube.

The exhausting honour you must pay your fragility.

But I can't just leave the orgy,
it would be rude and if I do,
I'm back to being that shy little coward you fucked into a lover,
which renders every moment I had with you pointless,
doesn't it?

So I stay present with my permission to want,
grab the flesh of the nearest willing stranger
and try to focus on the journey,
rather than the destination,
of a single bed in a grimy hostel dorm,
in this city where you are somewhere.

Every tube ride I'm devastated that I didn't bump into you,
equally terrified I might,
now you're moved in with the girlfriend I saw on your phone,
when though you were there with me, for me,
you really just wanted to go home
because I was becoming hard work,
failing at not crying and trying not to beg.

See I never got to practice these unspoken protocols,
I had to fast track or die.
I don't know how to be politely satisfied when I'm ravenous,
when the invisible of me is finally seen.

I stay until someone starts to pump my pussy
with their fingers like a jackhammer.
Do my best not to indulge the fear
that you have indeed ruined me for all other men.
If I'll ever be able to wank without crying now,
but it was all totally worth it,
I'd do it all over again and thank god I can't.

Because the only way I could bring myself to jump back in,
was to fantasise that one day you might get back in touch,
proving my tentative hope
that I did mean something more to you and I'll tell you I did this,
went to an orgy, alone.
Didn't even bother with dating apps or singles bars,
just jumped right into kink events
and fetish munches and swinging.
When I finally worked up the nerve to actually join in,

I touched another woman's boobs and everything
and it was all very useful,
as exhilarating as it was disappointing.

And you'll laugh and tell me how proud you are of me,
for being so brave.

# New Stars

Tonight I am caterpillar soup,
melted down to the bones,
all my blind panic calmed.

You are my reward for
embracing unknowns,
handing myself over.

How will I ever give you up?
Thrive without this sunlight?

The idea of romance always made me shudder.
Even when I craved connection,
I wanted the mortifying misunderstandings,
so it felt safe.

I was prepared for an arrogant fuck boy.
But when you rubbed your forehead cat-like
against mine in a moment of post-coital bliss,
laughed at the way I held my pinky up as I sipped Processo,
"So English",
When you turned my head and said "Look at me"
and I drank you in and you saw me,
I finally felt alive.
Started to appreciate
why my friends told me not to go too deep,
knowing it would make no difference.

If I'd had the usual normal presumed
backlog of break ups and one night stands,
crying in nightclubs toilets because he didn't text back,
if I'd had all that,
maybe I'd be more prepared for this onslaught.
But I'm assured by those who know,
it doesn't get any easier.
All grief,
like love,
eventually brings you here,
to the bittersweet,
yet what's one but proof of the other?

That's why I welcome it,
vulnerability,
scared yet glowing
under the drug of your delight in me,
the chemistry I knew you weren't faking.
Though it doesn't change the fact that I paid for you,
nor the fact that my heart is breaking.

Like all those sighing lovers I resented,
secretly envied,
I too am stuck in expectant reluctance,
ready for the next encounter
that I both hope for and dread.

So I will savour you as we are now,
all oily slickness and animal passion,
then let it go,
grateful for every chance to soar
and singe true wings on new stars.

# Desire

So exquisitely have you wounded me with desire
I could tear you apart and fall at your feet.
That there are men like you,
that can hand a woman back to herself so instinctively,
like it's nothing
and that I can't keep you,
is a brutal intricate liberation I can't resolve.
That explodes the body quietly,
leaves me full with emptiness and angry want.
Desire is the raising of an old story buried deep
into the heights of the sublime,
but I never could walk in high heels without stumbling,
feeling like mutton dressed as lamb.

Never was I more powerful than
when I got on my knees,
I'd just been waiting for someone worthy,
that would never ask unless I expressed a need.
Power equaled only by my cyclic helplessness,
as if it never happened.
As if you never sank your teeth into my flesh,
surprised by my serene command for more, harder.
Desire is a pretty bruise I keep squeezing as it fades,
begging just stay,
stay with me a little longer.

Sometimes I wish I could rip it out of me,
the life saving fire of you,
the pulse that makes me yearn.

That won't just let me die back to that black and white world
I could understand,
though it crushed my lungs.
Now I know what I'm missing,
it's all electric thunderstorms and exquisite rainbows.
Desire is all weather and no mercy.

I am scared lover,
that your freedom has ruined me,
that I am still too much and not enough,
that I only got to feast on this banquet because I paid for it
and overspent on the first touch.
Desire is an enemy saviour,
always slithering insubstantial out of my hands
and still somehow overwhelming.

Desire is a beautiful terrible perfect mess,
full of complete immediate joy
and anguished aftermath.
I can't have one without the other,
I must navigate anguished joy.

Honour this truth
unraveled out of me unbidden,
because there's no filtering out
the fine aching scratch of it.

Abundance and scarcity churn together in my guts,
stabbing then stroking at the heart
in a dance I never learnt to master.
You are the dangerous thing now,
in place of the fear you fucked out of me.

Desire is a bowl of rubies and fishhooks,
but if we don't dip our hands in eagerly with our eyes closed,
why be alive?

Desire has made me brave in my quivering fragility,
naked in my best disguise,
greedy in my apologetic tongue bites,
fearless in my pursuit to disintegrate shame.
Yet, when asked by the curious,
I still can't say your name.

# Fuck Buddha

There are days when I think,
Buddha was such a typical man.
"Desire is the root of all suffering, remain neutral"

That he obviously never got laid,
or found women too mysterious,
their pleasures too complex.
Detachment from negative drama is noble,
but I say suck the marrow of desire dry.
What else makes all this horribleness bearable?
I say cleave to desire even as it drowns you.
It's so cold and boring to merely float through life and watch.
Why have a body at all if it never gets touched?

Then I have days like this one,
crushed by the night before.
Another one of those new age orgies
I now frequent because I'm so liberated,
where no one saved me
when I fell into the pit of social anxiety,
so I remained unfucked and unsatisfied,
hating that I need to be rescued at all,
knowing bullying myself into a Tinder profile
will only make it worse.

That I just don't have the necessary bravado,
to stop devouring myself.

And I think,
Buddha was right about everything.

I should just drag myself to another
silent ten day meditation retreat,
strangle this slippery viper of want once and for all,
so I can sit empty and victorious on my lotus flower,
compassionately smug in my spiritual bliss.

The trouble is,
desire doesn't care what kind of day I'm having,
regardless of my arrogance or my despair.
She just leans back on her plush velvet throne,
smirks knowingly like a 1920's vamp,
spreads her legs, tosses her gorgeous blazing hair and says,
"Well Buddha's come and go honey,
but I'm not going anywhere,
fuck Buddha"

# Freedom

I was the one with the keys as I sat in the cage,
half content,
half seething with unnameable fury.

I was the one holding the knife,
as my eyes darted through the bars,
seeing predators in passersby.

I was the one in my own way,
crashing into my fear over and over,
shaking my fists at the unfairness
of the whole stinking world.

Then,
I pushed the writhing exhale out of my lungs,
I pulled my shoulders down where they should be,
I repaid my heart for its naked exposure.

You,
lover for a borrowed season,
were the catalyst
the witness,
the touch stone.

Now I'm full blown butterfly,
smacking clumsy glittering wings at the world,
daring to land,
trusting I drink nectar,
hoping I only attract beauty
before my times up.

Revelling in tremoring aliveness,
I saw how all sex, nature, spirit, creativity
is one big cosmic fuck from the universe,
honed between two vessels truly empty of everything but light.

Now I fizz with shamelessness.
Lie back and trust the sun to find me under the canopy.

Now I know what I am worth.

# Brave

The bravest thing I've ever done wasn't hiring you,
or performing a show about my broken vagina,
or going to an orgy alone.
It wasn't even telling you on our last night together,
that I wasn't in love but felt like my heart was breaking,
knowing we both knew it was a contradiction.
That for all my compartmentalising,
I was probably lying,
that I was a little naïve for trying to keep you.
It's just that you made me brave
and that's not putting you on a pedestal.
Because I was never brave before,
it's not something I lost.
It was a flame that was doused out
before I even knew the word for fire.
You helped me find it, own it.

The bravest thing I've ever done is what I'm doing now.
Terrified of getting my heart truly broken,
but keeping it open anyway.
Resisting the urge to crawl back into the chrysalis,
because what's the point in flying solo,
if I can't have that moment of bliss on repeat?
It's not making myself go to sex clubs,
pretending I want to be a slapper,
rather than admit the embarrassment
that I just want to meet my prince.

Scrap that,
my King.
I know I am a Queen now,
you unearthed my forgotten sovereignty.
So I say goodbye to you now in these words,
because a page can give me dignity.
Thank you,
stranger, lover,
for everything.

And I say to my future lover,
lovers,
don't be strangers,
come find me.
But know I am not to be taken lightly.
I take my desire, my pleasure, my love
very seriously and I'm done apologising for my sensitivity.
I'm not a nurse,
a therapist,
a proxy mother,
a grateful spinster,
I am a lover.
What that turns me on the most
is being seen in my fragility.
What defines love for someone
whose always been on the outside of it,
is equality, honesty,
and honestly,
I don't love quietly,
moderately,
I'm all in and greedy in my generosity.
But know I'm still scared,
but more scared of me than I am of you,
the deeper journey into myself

that you might lead me to.
So let's dance,
I'm clumsy but enthusiastic.
Let's talk, all night,
about everything and nothing.
Let's teach the patriarchy the way of Eros and Psyche,
because I'm done with all this "love is pain" narrative tragedy.

Come find me in all my bumbling caterpillar innocence,
all my powerful unfurling butterfly beauty,
I'm ready.

# Cosmos

# Guts

This deep knowing down to the bones
is the only real certainty.
This fecundity pulsing in my cells made of stars,
the sliver of me attuned to the whole universe,
too vast to fathom with words.

So no more caging vitality.
Dousing my light
because others love their own darkness.
Spare me the illusion of safety.
Give me the raw ringing beauty
of my guts churning with risk and truth,
bright breathless risk for once,
not the worlds anesthetised identity crisis.
Not shoulders rolled around my coward heart,
never daring to exhale because I want too much.

I want to obliterate the existence of shame.

Make all wavering wishes burst alive with audacious desire.

Every sentient being bowled over by absolute ecstatic joy.

To just say it,
unfetter the tongue,
fade the scars of every bitten lip and pillow scream
on all otherwise brave ravenous hearts.

To stand tall,
breath deep.

My festering secret is now my talisman,
a lighthouse that makes fear cower
when I call it by its name.

I want to ride the sky
free of thought
limbs taut with life
knuckles white with danger
breath stolen by wind
body rocked by ancient rhythm.
Only sweat, muscles and focus
the horizon that keeps going
the ground that won't remember me.

There is no algorithm
that can predict my constancy.
Don't think you know anything about me
if I don't feel it in my guts,
that are not to be ripped out,
splayed over the altar,
probed for prophecy.

I am the stumbling definer of my own destiny.

# Two Wolves

There's something I never understood about those two wolves.
The one full of joy and love,
the other full of anger and greed
and the one that thrives is the one that you feed,
so feed the good wolf.

But what about the other one
that will only die lonely and rejected?
Whose stench isn't going to go away.
Why not give your worst fear half your hope to gnaw on,
to make it clean and purposeful?
Why not let it bask in the sun despite all your mistrust?
So it can learn to lie still without expecting danger.

Turn from the wild and it has to bite you
to bring you back to yourself.
We are animals who need the dirt
as much the diamonds.
The rage as much as the rainbows.

Why make your shadow starve?
as if its struggle,
its darkness,
its hunger,
has nothing to teach you.

# A Starling Sang in Birmingham City Centre

You are my favourites.

Each time I have to trudge through this city,
the streets full of preachers on speakers,
the stink of chicken shops,
I seek you out and you always
stop me in my tracks.

Your iridescent blues and greens,
a natural art show amidst the grime.
Your feet always moving,
eyes darting,
up to something.
Chancing it outside the Peaky Blinders bar in packs,
showing them real swagger.
Hovering around Greggs and Mac Donald's,
you know where the good stuff is,
crumbs on tap.
Always cocking your head cheekily for more,
"You've got a whole sausage roll there missy, keep it coming"

One particularly dismal day,
when my head was full of snagging blackness,
you reminded me why I'm alive.

I clocked two women filming one of you on their phones.
A particularly vocal member of your colourful tribe,
giving it some serious warbling on the scaffolding,
as if serenading a lady love.

I was enchanted too
and none of us cared about the teenagers skulking past,
rolling their eyes,
we knew we were witnessing something special.

Finally,
I thought,
someone else has looked up and noticed,
to love you like you should be loved.

# Barefoot Soul

To walk this earth with no shoes.
No pain from ill-fitting purchases
that never loosen up,
or clash with clumsy clothes.
That scuff and scrape at your heels,
when all you want is to stomp on unhindered.

To be free on the ground,
dirt between the digits,
skin hard enough to withstand the broken glass
of dreams scattered over drab paving slabs of boredom.
Soft enough to stop you in your tracks,
as you glide over grass
and remember when you didn't need any answers.

To walk this earth with no weight,
arms free of past straps and future freeloading,
limbs pliable as wet clay.
To end the day unrecognisable
from the tidiness of the morning.
To be free of the need to decide
which mask will do for the day?
To spin around your fiery urge to topple the blocks
until they crumble to chaos.
To jab mischievous fingers into the ribs of reality
until it rears its real face,
teeth blazing.

To walk this earth moved only
by the need to feel fulfilled inside.
No treasures to protect with threat.

To stand as calm on jagged rocks as you do on sand,
to carry only that which fits the palm of your hand,
to trust the tide and let the waves roll.
To walk this earth with no shoes,
with a shameless barefoot soul.

# Get Zen

*Written after a silent ten day Vipassana Meditation retreat*


It's not until the volume is turned down you realise,
the only real peace is between the inhale and the exhale.
The rest is just noise.

I'm learning something I forgot I always knew,
something profoundly simple,
it's not just the world that's spinning,
it's you.

It spins so slow your spine barely feels the shudder,
you spin until your agitated cells burst at the core.
So much time spent splitting yourself in two,
when in the end there is only you,
only silence to tell you how to be,
in a world designed to make a mockery of your subtlety.
It's not life that trips up your plans,
it's your too eager feet,
stumbling at stop signs,
tangled in train tracks,
rushing to squeeze all your hunger through closing doors
that can only crush your bones.

Know you are not at the end of the grinding wheel,
gripping tighter as it accelerates faster
with your only choice being to let go.

You are the still point at the centre,
who decides which turns matter
and if the wheel ever spins again,

only you know.
I'm trying not to pick at the answers
because to even ask the questions take longer.
The silence is breaking me but will put me back together
stronger.

I'm exploring the universe inside and it is vast.
Every cell has its own story,
every muscle its own past.
When I concentrate hard enough,
the tension in my neck suddenly cracks
and for the first time in years,
my shoulders are down where they should be.

Fall.
That's what the silence says to me.
If you shatter, fracture, falter,
I will put you back together.
Cell by cell I will carry you to shelter,
reconstruct you Isis-like,
made whole again with the patience of love.
Fall, I will catch you.
Don't hold back,
soar fearless.
There are oceans to drown mistakes in a heartbeat.
Eternity is played out in an eye blink and you're gone.
Catastrophes might as well be stars,
so far away and smudged out by a finger.
All there is is endlessness,
that ebbs and flows,
raindrops to sea,
seeds to tree,
babes to bones.
The fear is from the world,

it's not mine
and it's not that nothing ever happens,
it's that everything happens all at once all the time.

It's how you feel about the planets that orbit under your skin,
the comets that burn up your best laid plans,
the chaos you know you chose.
the earth shook
and its true treasures rose.

You forget to breath,
then you wonder why you can't breathe.
You do things that make no sense
then wonder why you make no sense.
Just breathe
and learn to love your silence.
If you don't learn to love your silence
it will wither under the noise
and you will cease to function without noise,
you will eat noise crave noise mind mangled noise,
aching down to your bones for someone else and all their
noise,
it's just noise.

Just turn it down,
breathe,
be.
What else has ever given you total clarity?

Breathe
just be
the rest is just noise.

# Goddess

*Inspired by the Exhibition 'Feminine Power: the divine to the demonic' at the British Museum, 2022*


We are the magic cunning of mother Isis.
We are Pele's erupting rage when you take from us
that which isn't yours.
We are Aphrodite's shameless sexuality,
pink and glistening,
so bow and ask with reverence.

We are Lilith's unblinking defiant gaze,
well may you fear us for seeing you fully
and walking away unimpressed.
We are Kuan Yin's gentle overwhelming compassion,
transforming fear into flowers.
We are the joyful salacious hip swinging of Oshun,
where we stamp the ground fountains burst forth.

We are the screaming but still dreaming deep red earth of Gaia.
The absolute 'Fuck you' of Kali in all her creative chaos
and you better run because she doesn't bluff.
We are Innanna's fearless descent into death,
emerging from the underworld with arms full
of Persephone's spring,
bursting forth with every breath.

We are pure love, seething fire and the balancing flood.

We are Danu's first spark and last exhale
before the whole bloody and beautiful cycle starts again,

So know this,
like Hecate we will fill the sky with crows
when you call us to wars we did not start.
We will take aim like Artemis,
unleash our snarling Sekhmet fury,
rain down Shakti's vibrant stars of true power,
hold the new world in our arms and
nurture with Mother Mary love,
all the damage done.

See us in all our unapologetic glory,
know we are thoroughly done with your fuckery.
And we will give you back your half of this world we co-created
before you got greedy,
when you are sorry, ready and worthy.

# Cosmos

I feel the planet of me spinning inside
since I started looking up.
Since quakes shook my rigid fault lines free,
so I had to nurture my fragility
like matter wraps around the void to make it sing.

It explains a lot,
this macro micro view.
The collision of forces between mind and heart,
beyond my control but at my mercy.
The sporadic meteor showers,
spit second overloads of catastrophe.

The suns blinding constancy
though like every star it's just dying slowly.

It accounts for the black holes,
the gaps of dense heaviness between the shining bodies.
That no-thing where all my hope gets sucked in,
no language left.

If I could map the trajectory of these killer comets,
I could spin on a perfect axis.
But these implosions are so beautiful.

Full of new life,
base metals,
precious jewels from a far cosmos,
that feels more like home than here.

All essential elements
for transformation.

# Waking Up

It took a doctor with her meat cleaver mouth saying the
unthinkable and how could I have forgotten, she says these words
to someone every day?

It took another awkward fumbling on his dog haired sofa, twenty
years later when I should have known better because he's still
a selfish prick who sees me as a hole, a joke, but he is now
transparent where once he felt heavy.

It took Sertraline and Diazepam and Zopiclone and talking to a
lovely old Christian councillor about my broken vagina and my
conflicted BDSM fantasies.

It took anger, finally. The anger at her betrayal that I'd forgotten
until the dirt hit the coffin lid and I would never get an
explanation. Knowing it was never that I wasn't capable, it was
just waiting, a cornered wounded animal ready to tear the world
down. That it's essentially healthy in its drive to build a scaffold
around your throat for you to climb and exclaim with perfect
entitlement, "Fuck This Shit"

It took you, the man I chose, the man I ordered off the internet to
"save me" from myself, from her ghost, kissing my neck so I
wriggled with joy, rewarding me for my honest neurosis with clit
licks, whipping my shame out of me with my express permission
and I never felt scared, stranger, not for a single moment of it. I
told her ghost I forgave her snuggled up against your beautiful
body and I meant it.

It took traumatised horses returning my gentle nose blows to
make friends as if to say, "I get it."

It took colouring in flowers at the table while my friends talked about films and all the time the words "kill yourself" went round and round in my head and how could I explain when it made no sense to me? If I just ignore it long enough, if I just acknowledge it long enough. It went away but it still scares me.

It took barefoot soul sister womb healing earth worship with total conviction, trust and pride.

It took all this vicious cerebral gorgeous crashing together of sublime destruction and benign fury unleashed to snap me out of trying to be behave rather than claiming desire.

To stop expecting the world to tell me who I am.

To unravel me into a natural state of grace.

A woman who can say cunt without stammering or apologising.

Who can dance like she's about to die with her eyes closed, arms out wide, trusting the chaos.

Because it's no longer good enough to just survive.

Live,
says the messy scar undulating in spirals inside my heart,
the ghost of bite marks on my neck where I was resurrected,
the voice of mother earth soothing the rage,
live
live
live
thrive.

Look up daughter and never look down again.

# ACKNOWLEDGEMENTS

The poems in Brazen are taken from my autobiographical solo show of the same name about my obsession with Jim Morrison, my coming of age, the complexities of idolatry and the transformative power of music. The show previewed at Birmingham Theatre Festival and was live-streamed from the Arena Theatre, Wolverhampton.

Tight and Sacred featured in my second solo NO ENTRY! about my experience of Vaginismus, the toxicity around the concept of virginity and transmuting sexual shame. It had a sell out show at the 'Calm Down Dear' Feminist Theatre Festival at Camden Peoples Theatre.

Most of the poems in A Virgins Guide to Hiring an Escort are the content of my live theatrical poem cycle of the same name. All three shows are available on my Youtube Channel: https://www.youtube.com/@LornaRosePoet

Feast was featured in Anansi Archive's Anthology *The Nine Lives of Billy Nightjar*, edited by Dave Jordan.

Wild Swim was chosen to be in the 'Life Wonders' Anthology commissioned by Rhianna Levi, Poet Laureate of Worcester 2022-2023, published by Black Pear Press in aid of Worcestershire Acute Hospitals Charity. https://blackpear.net/print-and-ebooks/

A Starling Sang in Birmingham City Centre was part of the Hope Central soundscape art project curated by Rick Saunders (aka Willis the Poet) which in turn inspired a beautiful art work by Rachel Massey: www.rachelmassey.co.uk

THANK-YOUS

Massive thanks and big loves to:

Giovanni Esposito for being a consistent confidence builder, mentor, collaborator, editor and the Punk Uncle I never had.

Dreadlockalien, Bohdan Piasecki and Emma Purshouse for making the Birmingham poetry scene so prolific, inclusive and awesome and for always making me feel like I had a place in it.

Max Easey, Nina Lewis and Holly Daffurn for looking at early drafts and editing suggestions.

The Decadent Diva's for years of laughing, homemade soup, poems about wobbly bits and for one of the best gigs of my life at Ledbury Poetry Festival.

Kim, Claire, Jane, Gerri, Elinor, Tracy and all my other soul sisters who bigged me up, picked me up, got me through hell and listened patiently to all my vagina talk.

Serenah Cole for that auspicious Glastonbury ticket.

Zak Marsh for all the directing, technical wizardry, and tireless encouragement getting the solo shows out into the world.

Claire Tedstone for your gorgeous cover design and art work and totally getting what I meant when I said I wanted to be a cosmic butterfly goddess.

Stuart Bartholomew and VERVE Poetry Press for helping me build a legacy after twenty odd years in the poetry business.

## ABOUT VERVE POETRY PRESS

**Verve Poetry Press** is an award-winning press that focused initially on meeting a local need in Birmingham - a need for the vibrant poetry scene here in Brum to find a way to present itself to the poetry world via publication. Co-founded by Stuart Bartholomew and Amerah Saleh, it now publishes poets from all corners of the UK - poets that speak to the city's varied and energetic qualities and will contribute to its many poetic stories.

Added to this is a colourful pamphlet series, many featuring poets who have performed at our sister festival - and a poetry show series which captures the magic of longer poetry performance pieces by festival alumni such as Polarbear, Matt Abbott and Imogen Stirling.

*The press has been voted Most Innovative Publisher at the Saboteur Awards, and has won the Publisher's Award for Poetry Pamphlets at the Michael Marks Awards.*

Like the festival, we strive to think about poetry in inclusive ways and embrace the multiplicity of approaches towards this glorious art.

www.vervepoetrypress.com
@VervePoetryPres
mail@vervepoetrypress.com